Contents

Meets **Accreditation Standard** for Child-created Bulletin Boards

Unit 5: The Little Red Hen

Unit 6: Fourth, Flags, and Fun

Unit 7: Author Study— Paul Galdone

Three Cheers for June and July PreK–K, SV 9826-4

Introduction

This series of monthly activity books is designed to give PreK and Kindergarten teachers a collection of hands-on activities and ideas for each month of the year. The activities are standards-based and reflect the philosophy that children learn best through play. The teacher can use these ideas to enhance the development of language and math skills, and of social/emotional and physical growth of children. The opportunity to promote pre-reading skills is present throughout the series and should be incorporated whenever possible.

Organization and Features

This book consists of seven units:

Unit 1 provides reproducible pages and information for the months in general.
- newsletter outlines to promote parent communication
- blank thematic border pages
- a list of special days in the months
- calendar ideas to promote math skills
- blank calendar grids that can also be used as incentive charts

Units 2–6 include an array of activities for five **theme** topics. Each unit includes
- teacher information on the theme
- arts and crafts ideas
- a food activity
- poetry, songs, and books
- bulletin board ideas
- center activities correlated to specific learning standards

Implement the activities in a way that best meets the needs of individual children.

Unit 7 focuses on a well-known **children's author**. The unit includes
- a biography of the author
- activities based on a literature selection
- a list of books by the author
- reproducible bookmarks

In addition, each book contains
- reproducible **icons** suitable to use as labels for centers in the classroom. The icons coordinate with the centers in the book. They may also be used with a work assignment chart to aid in assigning children to centers.
- reproducible **student awards**
- **calendar day patterns** with suggested activities

Research Base

Howard Gardner's theory of multiple intelligences, or learning styles, validates teaching thematically and using a variety of approaches to help children learn. Providing a variety of experiences will assure that each child has an opportunity to learn in a comfortable way.

Following are the learning styles identified by Howard Gardner.
- **Verbal/Linguistic** learners need opportunities to read, listen, write, learn new words, and to tell stories.
- **Musical** learners enjoy music activities.
- **Logical/Mathematical** learners need opportunities to problem solve, count, measure, and do patterning activities.
- **Visual/Spatial** learners need opportunities to paint, draw, sculpt, and create art works.
- **Interpersonal** learners benefit from group discussions and group projects.
- **Intrapersonal** learners learn best in solitary activities, such as reading, writing in journals, and reflecting on information.
- **Naturalist** learners need opportunities to observe weather and nature and to take care of animals and plants.
- **Existential** learners can be fostered in the early years by asking children to think and respond, by discussions, and journal writing.

Gardner, H. (1994). *Frames of mind*. New York: Basic Books.

June News

Teacher: _____   Date: _____

Headline News

Coming Up

Happy Birthday to

Special Thanks to

Help Wanted

Unit 1, Teacher Resources: Newsletter
Three Cheers for June and July PreK–K, SV 9826-4

July News

Teacher: _____ Date: _____

Headline News

Coming Up

Happy Birthday to

Special Thanks to

Help Wanted

Unit 1, Teacher Resources: Newsletter
Three Cheers for June and July PreK–K, SV 9826-4

June

July

Unit 1, Teacher Resources: Border Page
Three Cheers for June and July PreK–K, SV 9826-4

Special Days

June

Father's Day (Third Sunday in June)   Have children draw a picture of something they enjoy doing with their father or a special adult male.

Safety Month   Discuss summer safety practices, such as using sunscreen, riding bikes with proper equipment, and barbeque grills.

Zoo and Aquarium Month
Have children celebrate with activities from the Fishy Fish unit that begins on page 27.

5 World Environment Day
As you share the Summer unit with children, take time to discuss the need for clean water to drink, clean with, and play in. Invite children to draw a picture showing how they enjoy clean water in the summer and what they can do to keep it clean.

10 Maurice Sendak's Birthday   Read *Where the Wild Things Are* in honor of his birthday.

14 Flag Day   Have children look at an American flag and their state flag. Have them talk about how the flags are alike and different. Point out colors and shapes. Then challenge children to use shape blocks to create the flags.

17 Eat Your Vegetables Day   Ask children to bring to school a favorite vegetable. Provide plastic knives, ranch dressing, and bowls to make a huge salad to share.

23 National Pink Day   Provide a variety of art materials that are different shades of pink. Have children make a "Pink Day" collage.

28 Paul Bunyan Day   Read a tall tale about Paul Bunyan and his blue ox, Babe. Then invite children to tell a tall tale of their own about something wonderful that Paul and Babe could do together.

July

Anti-Boredom Month   Help children brainstorm a list of things they can do when they want to say "I'm bored!"

National Hot Dog Month   While the camping area is set up in the A-camping We Will Go! unit that begins on page 42, prepare hot dogs and invite children to sit around the campfire and eat them.

1 Creative Ice-Cream Flavor Day
Challenge children to think of the weirdest ice-cream flavor they can and share the flavor with the class during circle time.

3 Compliment Your Mirror Day   Discuss what a compliment is; then lead children to understand that when people compliment their mirror, they are complimenting the face in the mirror—themselves. Allow children to hold a hand mirror and say one nice thing about themselves.

4 Independence Day   Have children celebrate with activities from the Fourth, Flags, and Fun unit that begins on page 71.

9 National Sugar Cookie Day   Invite children to decorate store-bought sugar cookies with icing and small candies.

25 Threading the Needle Day   Using a large-eyed plastic needle, have children thread it with yarn and sew shapes in burlap fabric squares.

28 Karla Kushkin's Birthday   Read some poems by this poet to children in order to celebrate her birthday.

31 Parent's Day   Have children dictate a sentence telling something special their parents do for them and draw a picture to illustrate it.

June

Sunday	Monday	Tuesday	Wednesday	Thursday	Friday	Saturday

Three Cheers for June and July PreK–K, SV 9826-4

July

Sunday	Monday	Tuesday	Wednesday	Thursday	Friday	Saturday

Unit 1, Teacher Resources: July Calendar
Three Cheers for June and July PreK–K, SV 9826-4

Calendar Activities for June and July

Classroom Calendar Setup

The use of the calendar in the classroom can provide children with daily practice on learning days, weeks, months, and years. As you plan the setup for your classroom, include enough space on the wall to staple a calendar grid labeled with the days of the week. Leave space above the grid for the name of the month and the year. Next to the calendar, staple twelve cards labeled with the months of the year and the number of days in each month. Leave these items on the wall all year. At the beginning of each month, start with the blank calendar grid. Do not staple anything on the grid that refers to the new month. Leave the days of the week and the year in place.

Introducing the Months of June and July

Before children arrive, gather all of the items that will go on the calendar for that month. You may want to include the following:
- name of the month
- number cards
- name cards to indicate birthdays during the month
- picture cards that tell about special holidays or school events during the month
- a small treat to be taped on the day of each child's birthday. You may wish to gift wrap the treat.

Add a special pointer that can be used each day while doing calendar activities. See page 12 for directions on how to make special pointers for both June and July. Place these items in a picnic basket. Select a puppet that can remain in the basket and come out only to bring items for each new month. A dog puppet works well because of the large mouth which makes it easier to grasp each item.

On the first school day of the month, follow this procedure:

1. Place the picnic basket in front of the class. Pull out the puppet and introduce it to children if it is the first time they have seen it or ask them if they remember why the puppet is here. If this is the first time they have seen it, explain that the puppet will visit on the first day of each month to bring the new calendar items.

2. Have the puppet pull out the name of the month. According to the abilities of children, have them name the first letter in the name of the month, count the letters, or find the vowels. Staple the name of the month above the calendar.

3. Have the puppet pull out the new pointer for the teacher or the daily helper to use each day during calendar time.

4. Next, pull out the number cards for the month. You may use plain number cards, cards made from the calendar day pattern on page 96, or seasonal die-cut shapes. By using two or three die-cut shapes, you can incorporate building patterns as part of your daily calendar routine.

5. Place the number one card or die-cut under the day of the week on which the month begins. Locate June or July on the month cards that are stapled next to your calendar. Have children tell how many days this month will have and then count that many spaces on the calendar to indicate the end of the month. You may wish to place a small stop sign as a visual reminder of the end of the month. Save the remaining numbers cards or die-cut shapes and add one each day.

6. If there are any birthdays during the month, have the puppet pull out of the basket the cards that have a birthday symbol with the child's name and birth date written on it. Count from the number 1 to find where to staple this as a visual reminder of each child's birthday. If you have included a wrapped treat for each child, tape it on the calendar on the correct day.

7. Finally, have the puppet bring out cards that have pictures of holidays or special happenings, such as field trips, picture day, or story time in the library. Staple the picture cards on the correct day on the calendar grid. You can use these to practice various counting skills such as counting how many days until a field trip, a birthday, or a holiday.

8. When the basket is empty, say goodbye to the puppet and return it to the picnic basket. Put the basket away until the next month. Children will look forward to the beginning of each month in order to see what items the puppet will bring for the class calendar.

Making a June Sun Pointer

Include a June sun pointer in the calendar basket for this month. To make a pointer, you will need the following:
- two 3" sun shapes cut from poster board
- a medium-sized dowel rod that is 18" long
- several 12" lengths of narrow green and yellow ribbons

Directions:
1. Hot-glue the ribbons to the end of the dowel rod so that they lie against the rod.
2. Hot-glue the two sun shapes to the end of the dowel rod so that the sun shapes cover the glued ends of the ribbons.

The calendar helper can use this to point to the day of the week, the number, the month, and the year as the class says the date each day.

Making a July Star Pointer

Follow the directions above for making the sun pointer but replace the sun shape with a star shape and use red, white, and blue ribbons. You may wish to cover the star with silver glitter.

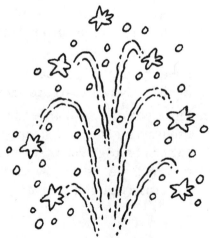

Three Cheers for June and July PreK–K, SV 9826-4

The Scoop on Summer

 The Eiffel Tower in France grows almost six inches each summer. The heat from the sun causes the metal to expand.

 Some stories say that the ice-cream cone was invented during the 1904 St. Louis Exposition when a waffle vendor made rolled waffles for the ice-cream vendor, who had run out of dishes. Actually, an immigrant started selling cones in 1896 when people kept taking his glass dishes. The man patented the idea in 1903.

 The first ice cream was actually a flavored ice eaten by ancient Roman elites. Slaves went to the mountains to get snow and ice to make the sweet food.

 It takes about 50 licks of the tongue to eat a single scoop of ice cream.

 The first day of summer is June 21, also known as the "summer solstice." The North Pole is tilted more toward the sun than at any other time of the year.

 Summer solstice is the time when the sun is the highest in the sky, resulting in about 15 hours of daylight for most people on the North American continent.

 The North Pole gets 24 hours of daylight at this time, while the South Pole gets 24 hours of darkness.

 The true origin of the hot dog is unknown. Some believe Frankfurt, Germany, was the birthplace of the "frankfurter." Others believe Vienna (Wien), Austria, was the birthplace of the "wiener." By 1600, the food was called "dachshund sausages."

 The term "hot dog" is certainly an American invention. Stories say that vendors were hawking the hot dachshund sausages on a cold day. A reporter did not know how to spell *dachshund*, and called them "hot dogs" instead.

 Early explorers carved out watermelons and used them as canteens.

Unit 2, Summer: Teacher Information
Three Cheers for June and July PreK–K, SV 9826-4

Sun Visor

Materials

- large paper plates
- markers
- stapler
- scissors

Directions

Teacher Preparation: Cut the circular centers out of the plates, leaving the outer rim to make the visor bands. Cut across the visor band to have two ends. Cut the inner circles in half to make visor bridges. After children decorate their visor parts, help them staple the visor bridge over the cut line of the band so that the visor bands fit snugly on their heads.

1. Use markers to decorate one visor band and one visor bridge.

2. Fit the band on the head and staple the ends together.

3. Line up the flat edge of the bridge with the inner part of the band and staple the two pieces together.

Sunflowers

Materials

- pattern on page 22
- large paper plates
- sunflower seeds
- yellow construction paper
- sponge brushes
- liquid glue
- containers
- newspaper
- scissors
- hot glue gun and glue
- carpet or decorator fabric tubes
- green and yellow tempera paints

Directions

Teacher Preparation: Trace several petal patterns on a sheet of paper and duplicate multiple copies on yellow paper. Set up a place where children can spread newspapers on the floor to paint the tubes. Heat the glue gun out of the reach of the children.

1. Paint the outside of a tube with the green tempera paint to be the sunflower stem.

2. Paint the paper plate with the yellow tempera paint to be the sunflower head.

3. Spread a layer of glue in the center of the paper plate.

4. Press sunflower seeds into the glue.

5. Cut out enough petals to fit around the paper plate.

6. Glue the petals around the rim of the plate and set the plate aside to dry.

7. Get help from an adult to hot glue the sunflower head to the stem.

Ice-Cream Rolls

You will need

- milk
- sugar
- vanilla
- ice
- salt
- small, resealable plastic bags
- large coffee cans with lids
- measuring cups
- measuring spoons
- bowls
- spoons

Directions

Teacher Preparation: You may want children to work in pairs. Dispose of the salt water properly.

1. Measure one cup of milk and pour it into a plastic bag.

2. Add one tablespoon of sugar to the bag.

3. Add one-half teaspoon of vanilla to the bag.

4. Seal the bag and shake the mixture to dissolve the sugar.

5. Fill the coffee can half full with ice.

6. Put the bag in the coffee can.

7. Fill the can with ice.

8. Measure one-fourth cup of salt over the ice and seal the can.

9. Roll the can back and forth to a partner or take turns shaking the can for about 20 minutes.

10. When the mixture is frozen, serve it in bowls and enjoy eating it.

Note: Be aware of children who may have food allergies.

Summertime Fun

The sun is out.	(Arms form a circle above the head.)
It's time to play,	
And have some fun	(Spread arms open to the side.)
This summer day!	
We'll go for a swim.	(Pantomime swimming.)
We'll go for a hike.	(Pantomime walking.)
We'll play some ball,	(Pantomime hitting or tossing a ball.)
And ride a bike.	(Pantomime riding a bike.)
So come along	(Gesture toward the body.)
And play with me,	
To see how fun	(Spread arms open to the side.)
Summer can be!	

Make a Splash with These Books

D.W. All Wet
by Marc Brown (Little Brown & Company)

Froggy Learns to Swim
by Jonathan London (Viking Children's Books)

Grandma Summer
by Harley Jessup (Viking Children's Books)

Ice Cream
by Elisha Cooper (Greenwillow)

Ice Cream Larry
by Jill Pinkwater (Marshall Cavendish)

Maisy's Pool
by Lucy Cousins (Candlewick Press)

Summer Is . . .
by Charlotte Zolotow (Thomas Y. Crowell)

Summer's Vacation
by Greg Couch (Simon & Schuster)

The Summer Noisy Book
by Margaret Wise Brown
(HarperCollins Juvenile Books)

Time of Wonder
by Robert McCloskey (Puffin)

Enjoy a Slice of Summer Fun!

Materials

- patterns on page 23
- green, white, red, and black construction paper
- white drawing paper
- craft paper
- border
- scissors
- colors or markers
- glue
- stapler
- clean watermelon seeds (optional)

Directions

Teacher Preparation: Duplicate and cut out the watermelon pattern pieces: the shell is on green paper, the rind is on white paper, and the fruit is on red paper. Provide a rind, fruit, and shell for each student. Cover the board with the craft paper of your choosing. Add a festive border and the caption.

1. Glue the white rind on the green shell so that the straight edges match.

2. Glue the red fruit on the white rind so that the straight edges match.

3. Glue up to ten seeds on the fruit, or cut out oval seeds from black paper and glue them on the fruit.

4. On a white sheet of paper, draw a picture of your face that is as big as the watermelon slice.

Help children count the seeds on their watermelon slices. Then staple the watermelon slices below the children's faces on the board so that it looks like they are eating the fruit.

Three Cheers for June and July PreK–K, SV 9826-4

Summer Centers

Language Center

Language Arts Standard
Recognizes uppercase and lowercase letters

A Cool ABC

Materials

- patterns on page 22
- brown construction paper
- pale colors of construction paper

Teacher Preparation: Trace and cut out 26 cone patterns from brown paper. Write a capital letter from *A* to *Z* on the cones. Trace and cut out 26 ice-cream scoop patterns from the colored paper. Write a lowercase *a* to *z* on the scoops.

Invite children to match the capital letters to the lowercase letters to make ice-cream cones. You might also wish to have children make an ice-cream cone with 26 scoops of ice cream by having children alphabetize the letters.

Extension: For a phonemic awareness activity, draw or cut out pairs of pictures whose names rhyme. For example, cut out magazine pictures of a star and a car. Glue one picture on a cone and the other on a scoop. Children match the rhyming pictures.

Math Center

Math Standard
Compares amounts

More Summer Fun

Materials

- crayons
- activity master on page 24

Teacher Preparation: Duplicate the activity master.

Have children color the picture in each group that can hold more water.

Summer Centers

Sensory Center

Science Standard
Understands properties of objects

Sink or Float

Materials

- tub
- water
- a variety of items that can sink or float, such as a cork, sponge, soap, small pool toy, toy car, crayon, rock, penny, etc.

Teacher Preparation: Fill the tub with water.

Challenge children to predict which items will float and which will sink. Then have them check their predictions.

Science Center

Science Standard
Recognizes changes in Earth and sky

Summer Signs

Materials

- glue
- crayons
- scissors
- activity master on page 25

Teacher Preparation: Duplicate the activity master.

Have children color the pictures that show things they would most likely see in the summer. Have them cut apart the pictures and glue the summer pictures in the boxes.

Summer Centers

Writing Center

Summertime Is Fun Time

Materials

- crayons
- activity master on page 26

Teacher Preparation: Duplicate the activity master.

Have children draw a picture of a favorite summertime activity. Then have them dictate or write words to complete the sentence frame.

Art Center

Fly Away, Fly!

Materials

- tempera paints
- clean meat trays
- plastic flies (or pictures of flies)
- fly swatters (one for each color of paint)
- glue
- scissors
- craft paper
- clothespins

NOTE: This is a fun, but very messy activity. You may wish to do this activity on a day that the children bring swimsuits and another adult can help to supervise the outside fun.

Teacher Preparation: Cut the craft paper into two-foot squares. Use clothespins to pin the squares to a chain link fence. Pour paint into the trays and set a fly swatter in each.

Invite children to create pictures by swatting the paper with the different colors of paint. While the pictures dry, have children examine a plastic fly and identify its different parts. Then have children glue several flies to their pictures.

Summer Centers

Reading Center

Social Studies Standard
Identifies the human and physical characteristics of an environment

Vacation Station

Materials

- tape
- travel posters

Teacher Preparation: Tape the travel posters on the wall.

Have children look at the posters and choose a place they would like to visit. Challenge them to take turns giving clues about the places for a partner to guess.

Game Center

Math Standard
Demonstrates awareness of addition and subtraction in everyday life

Ice-Cream Fling

Materials

- construction paper
- pattern pieces on page 22
- clean ice-cream containers
- tape
- scissors
- beanbags

Teacher Preparation: Trace, cut out, and make ice-cream cones from the ice-cream cone pattern pieces to match the flavors on the containers. Tape the cones to the appropriate buckets. Then line the buckets up in a row, preferably next to a wall.

Point out that the paper cones on the buckets show the ice-cream flavors. Invite partners to each throw three beanbags into the bucket that is their favorite flavor. Then have them work together to find how many beanbags are in each bucket after everyone has had a turn.

Petal Pattern

Use with "Sunflowers" on page 14.

petal

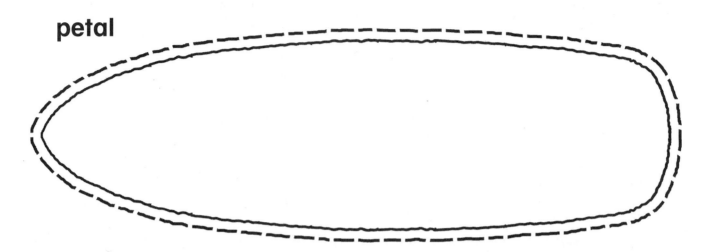

Ice-Cream Cone Pattern Pieces

Use with "A Cool ABC" on page 18 and "Ice-Cream Fling" on page 21.

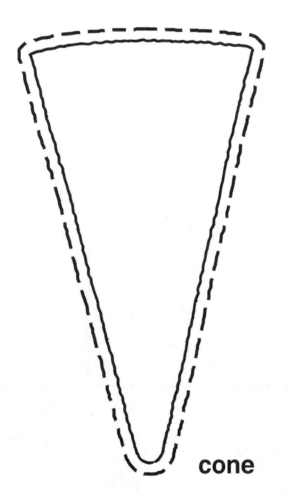

cone

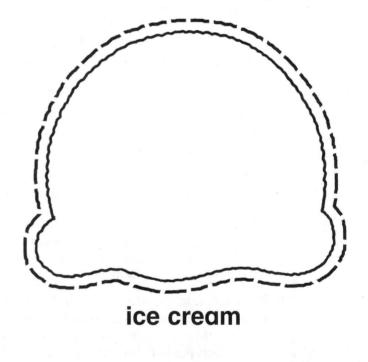

ice cream

Watermelon Pattern Pieces

Use with "Enjoy a Slice of Summer Fun" on page 17.

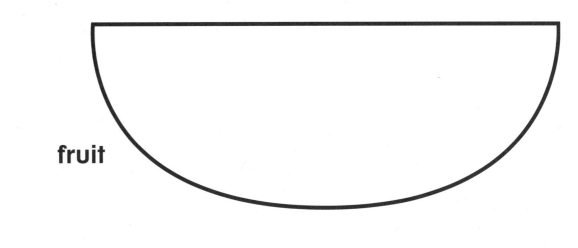

fruit

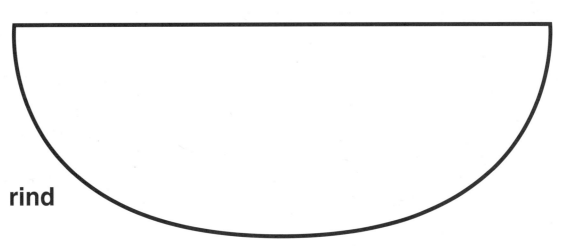

rind

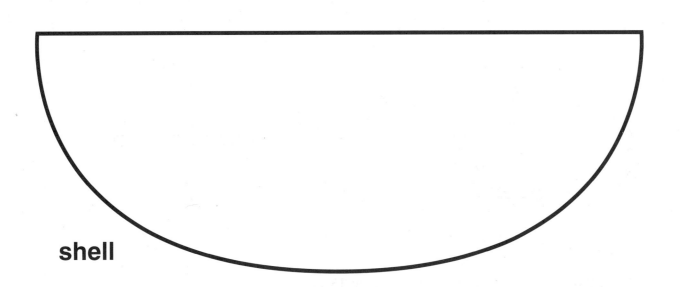

shell

Three Cheers for June and July PreK–K, SV 9826-4

Which Holds More?

1

2

3

Directions: Use with "More Summer Fun" on page 18. Have children color the picture in each group that can hold more water.

Name _____

I See Summer

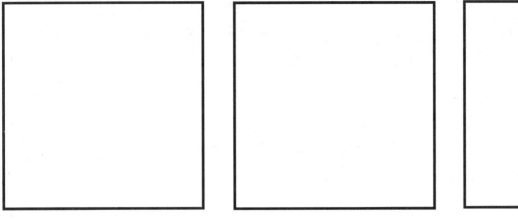

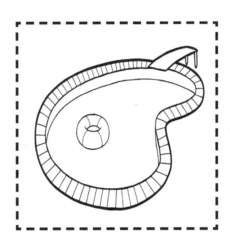

Directions: Use with "Summer Signs" on page 19. Have children color the pictures that show things they would most likely see in the summer. Have them cut apart the pictures and glue the summer pictures in the boxes.

Unit 2, Summer: Activity Master
Three Cheers for June and July PreK–K, SV 9826-4

Summer Fun

In the summer, I like to _____

_____

Directions: Use with "Summertime Is Fun Time" on page 20. Have children draw a picture of a favorite summertime activity. Then have them dictate or write words to complete the sentence frame.

Fishing for Facts

 The largest fish is the whale shark. It often grows to over 45 feet in length.

 Sharks swam in the ocean long before dinosaurs existed.

 The top and bottom of a fish's mouth moves, unlike most other animals.

 Sharks grow over 20,000 teeth in their lifetime.

 Sharks constantly grow teeth. A shark's tooth can be replaced every eight days.

Great white sharks can go almost three months without eating.

A shark does not have any bones in its body. It keeps its shape with cartilage, the flexible kind of material that is found in the nose.

 Fish can stay buoyant because of a swim bladder, a sack filled with gas in their abdomens.

 Fish are covered with scales. Fins and tails help them move through the water.

 Fish have gills that help them get the oxygen out of the water that they need to breathe.

 Many fish that live in the deepest parts of the ocean glow in the dark. This helps them see their prey and attract mates.

 The anglerfish has something on its head that looks like a fishing pole and worm. When small fish come near looking for food, the anglerfish eats them.

 A sea anemone looks like a plant, but it is really a fish. Its stinging tentacles resemble plant leaves.

 The clown fish lives in the tentacles of a sea anemone. The bright color of the clown fish attracts prey to the anemone. Bits of food dropped by the anemone become food for the clown fish. A thick coating on the clown fish keeps it from being stung by the anemone.

Puffy Fish Puppet

Materials

- patterns on page 36
- tag board
- small paper bags
- blue gift ribbon
- newspaper
- tempera paint
- craft sticks
- paintbrushes
- containers
- scissors
- stapler
- glue
- markers

Directions

Teacher Preparation: Trace several fish and fins patterns on tag board and cut them out. Provide patterns for each child.

1. Trace a fish body and a fin on a paper bag.

2. Cut the body and fin through all the thicknesses of the paper bag, making two fish.

3. Lay both fish on a table so that they are tail-to-tail and facing the opposite way.

4. Paint and decorate the fish so both sides are the same.

5. Paint and decorate the fins.

6. When they are dry, staple the bodies together, leaving an opening at the bottom. Stuff crumpled newspaper between the two bodies.

7. Glue on the fins.

8. Put glue on the end of a craft stick and slide it between the bodies for a puppet handle.

9. Glue strips of ribbon around the stick to look like water.

Scaly Fish

Materials

- pattern on page 37
- light blue construction paper
- bubble wrap
- tempera paints
- clean meat trays
- sponges
- markers
- scissors

Directions

Teacher Preparation: Duplicate the fish pattern on blue construction paper. Place a sponge in each tray and pour some paint over the sponge. Cut the bubble wrap into two-inch squares.

1. Press the bubble wrap on the sponge to get some paint.

2. Press the painted bubble wrap on the fish to print "scales."

3. Repeat the process several times to cover the fish in scales. Use different colors if desired.

4. When the paint is dry, add features with markers.

Going Fishing

You will need

- blue fruit juice
- long pretzel logs
- string licorice
- gummy worms
- gummy sharks
- tall, clear plastic cups

Directions

1. Tie a piece of string licorice on the end of a pretzel.
2. Tie a worm on the other end of the licorice.
3. Pour blue juice into a cup.
4. Put two or three gummy sharks in the cup.
5. Pretend to fish by dipping the worm into blue water.

Note: Be aware of children who may have food allergies.

Three Cheers for June and July PreK–K, SV 9826-4

♫ Five Little Fish Chant

Five little fish went out for a swim.

Across the water they jumped and skimmed.

The first fish said, "It's getting dark."

The second fish said, "I see a shark!"

The third fish said, "Hurry, let's hide!"

The fourth fish said, "His mouth is wide."

The fifth fish said, "He's gone at last."

Then the five little fish swam home really fast.

Extension

Have children work in groups of five and invite them to role-play the song using the puppets they made in "Puffy Fish Puppets" on page 28.

These Books Are Really Fishy!

Dolphins
by Silvia M. James (Mondo Pub)

Fish Eyes: A Book You Can Count On
by Lois Ehlert (Harcourt)

Fish Is Fish
by Leo Lionni (Dragonfly)

A Fish Out of Water
by Helen Palmer (Random House Books for Young Readers)

The Fish Who Could Wish
by John Bush and Corky Paul (KaneMiller)

The Rainbow Fish
by Marcus Pfister (North South Books)

One Fish Two Fish Red Fish Blue Fish
by Dr. Seuss (Random House Books for Young Readers)

Smiley Shark
by Ruth Galloway (Tiger Tales)

Swimmy
by Leo Lionni (Pantheon)

Surprising Shark
by Nicola Davies (Candlewick Press)

What's It Like to Be a Fish?
by Wendy Pfeffer (HarperTrophy)

Three Cheers for June and July PreK–K, SV 9826-4

Fishing for Help

Materials

- pattern on page 38
- fish (completed in "Scaly Fish" on page 28)
- white craft paper
- blue cellophane
- overhead projector
- transparency
- tempera paints
- border
- sponge brushes
- paint containers
- yarn
- pipe cleaner
- scissors
- stapler

Directions

Teacher Preparation: Make a transparency of the pattern. Cover the board with the craft paper. Use the transparency and overhead projector to trace a large boat and the girl on the bulletin board. Paint the boat and the girl. Use yarn to make a fishing line that drops into the water. Add a pipe cleaner hook. Add a festive border and the caption. Help children write their names on their fish and staple their fish below the boat. Then cover the fish with the cellophane to make water. Drape the hook on a fish to show which child will be the class helper that day or week.

Three Cheers for June and July PreK–K, SV 9826-4

Aquarium Centers

Math Center

Math Standard
Measures length using
nonstandard units

From Head to Tail

Materials

- patterns on page 39
- white correction fluid
- gray construction paper
- glue
- scissors
- file folder

Teacher Preparation: Duplicate the shark patterns and ruler on the gray paper. Cut out the sharks and the ruler. Glue the sharks on the inside of a folder. Vary the lengths so they are not in order. Then use the correction fluid to paint the teeth white.

Have children use the ruler to find out how many clips long each shark is.

Language Center

Language Arts Standard
Recognizes uppercase and
lowercase letters

ABC Fish

Materials

- hole punch
- 13 pipe cleaners
- pattern on page 37
- construction paper in a variety of colors
- 26 alphabet cards with uppercase and lowercase letters taped on a wall at children's level
- tape
- marker
- scissors

Teacher Preparation: Duplicate and cut out 26 fish patterns. Hole punch each fish. Write each pair of partner letters on separate fish. Cut the pipe cleaners in half and shape them into hooks. Tape a hook on each alphabet card on the wall so that the hook faces out.

Invite children to match each fish to the partner letters on the wall. Have children "hook" the fish to the card.

Aquarium Centers

 **Dramatic Play Center**

Language Arts Standard
Sequences events accurately

A Fishy Role-Play

Materials

- craft stick
- newspaper
- patterns on page 39
- gray construction paper
- blue and green streamers
- tape
- stapler
- scissors
- markers
- glue
- fish puppets (completed in "Puffy Fish Puppet" on page 28)

Teacher Preparation: Enlarge one of the shark patterns to fill a page. Then duplicate two copies of the shark on gray paper. Cut out the sharks and make a puffy shark puppet, following the directions in the "Puffy Fish Puppet" craft on page 28. Cut long lengths of the blue and green streamers so they reach from the ceiling to within two feet of the floor. Tape the streamers to the ceiling to make water and grass areas.

Review the "Five Little Fish" song (on page 30) with children. Then invite them to use their fish puppets and the shark puppet to role-play the song.

 **Puzzle Center**

Language Arts Standard
Recognizes sight words

Coloring Puzzle

Materials

- tag board
- activity master on page 40
- paper
- crayons

Teacher Preparation: Duplicate the activity master. Provide one for each child. Make a rebus chart on the tag board similar to the one on the top of the master to show which crayon colors match the words.

Point out the rebus color chart to the children. Have children color the crayons. Then have them color the picture.

Aquarium Centers

Art Center

Science Standard
Understands the characteristics of organisms

Shark Rubbings

Materials

- tag boards
- old scissors
- patterns on page 39
- crayons without covers
- glue
- newsprint
- sandpaper
- markers

Teacher Preparation: Enlarge the sharks and trace them on the backs of sandpaper. Cut out the sharks and glue them in various positions to pieces of tag board.

Explain to children that sharks have tiny scales that feel rough, like sandpaper. Then invite children to make crayon rubbings of the sharks on newsprint, using the length of different crayons. Invite children to add details to the rubbings.

Science Center

Science Standard
Recognizes the habitats of animals

In the Water

Materials

- scissors
- activity master on page 41
- glue
- crayons

Teacher Preparation: Duplicate the activity master.

Have children color the water scene. Then have them color the fish. Have them cut apart the pictures and glue the fish in the boxes.

Aquarium Centers

Sensory Center

Math Standard
Counts sets of objects

The Net Gain

Materials

- fish net
- sponges
- scissors
- tub
- water

Teacher Preparation: Fill the tub with water. Cut the sponges into fish shapes.

Invite children to use the net to catch the floating fish. Have them count the fish they catch.

Reading Center

Reading Standard
Uses a diagram for information

These Parts Are Fishy!

Materials

- pattern on page 37
- patterns on page 39
- markers
- craft paper

Teacher Preparation: Enlarge the fish pattern and the largest shark pattern on craft paper. Label the parts of each fish, including the tail, fins, gills, eye, and mouth.

Have children compare the fish and the shark. Ask them to read the labels and find the parts that are the same. Challenge children to discuss how the body parts are different on each fish, even though the names are the same.

Fish Puppet Patterns

Use with "Puffy Fish Puppet" on page 28.

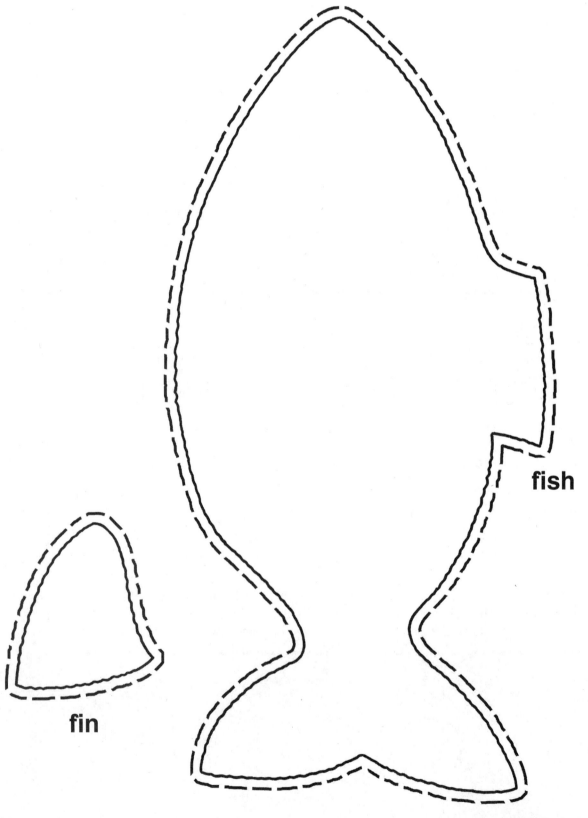

fish

fin

Three Cheers for June and July PreK–K, SV 9826-4

Fish Pattern

Use with "Scaly Fish" on page 28, "ABC Fish" on page 32, and "These Parts Are Fishy!" on page 35.

fish

Fishing Pattern

Use with "Fishing for Help" on page 31.

Three Cheers for June and July PreK–K, SV 9826-4

Shark Patterns
and Paper-Clip Ruler

Use with "From Head to Tail" on page 32, "A Fishy Role-Play" on page 33,
"Shark Rubbings" on page 34, and "These Parts Are Fishy!" on page 35.

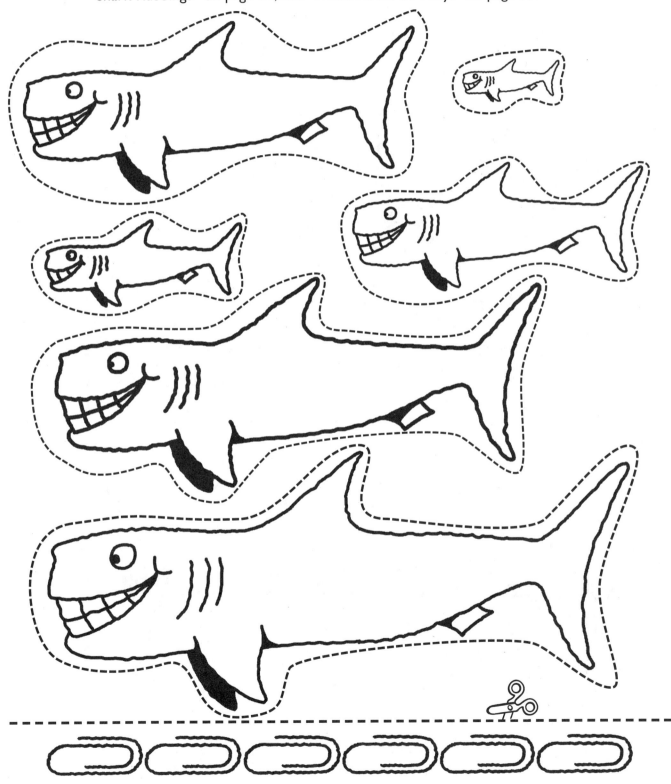

Three Cheers for June and July PreK–K, SV 9826-4

Name _____

What's Hiding?

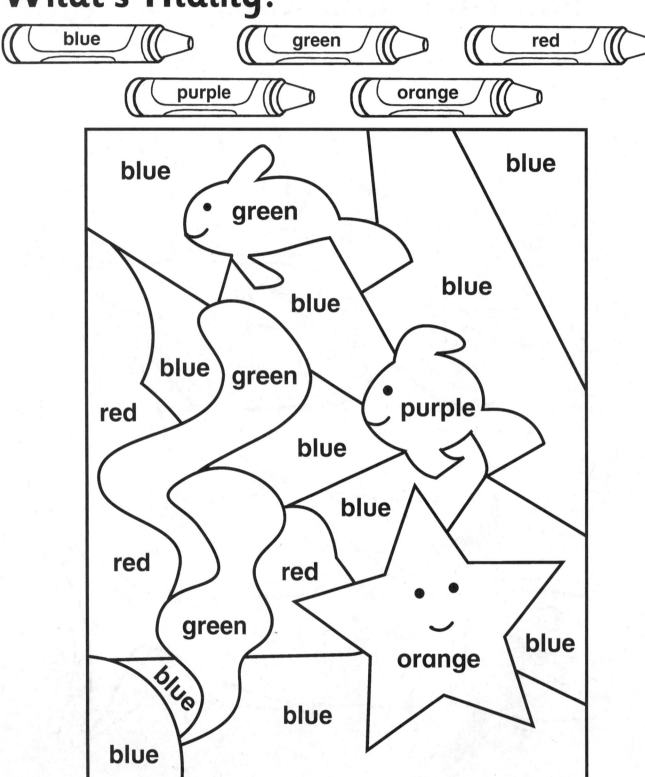

Directions: Use with "Coloring Puzzle" on page 33. Point out the rebus color chart to the children. Have children color the crayons. Then have them color the picture.

Unit 3, Fishy Fish: Activity Master
Three Cheers for June and July PreK–K, SV 9826-4

Name _____

Swim, Fish, Swim!

Directions: Use with "In the Water" on page 34. Have children color the water scene. Then have them color the fish. Have them cut apart the pictures and glue the fish in the boxes.

41

Unit 3, Fishy Fish: Activity Master
Three Cheers for June and July PreK–K, SV 9826-4

Some Camp News

 Binoculars are really two small telescopes joined together. The first working model was made in the mid-1800s.

 The canoe is an invention of the North American people. *Canoe* comes from the word *kenu*, which means *dugout*. The canoe is a kind of lightweight boat that is used to travel on water.

 The first canoes were made by people living in the Caribbean who cut down trees and carved out the inside.

 The Native Americans designed the canoes that are still popular today. They needed more lightweight transportation, so they used wood to make the skeleton, or ribs, of the boat. Then they covered it with tree bark.

 Tents have been used as shelters in many parts of the world, especially by nomadic people and by those involved in war. Tents were easy to move and light to carry.

 Tents were made with materials people found on the land. People used trees and animal bones for poles. Animal skins, woven wool, and silk were used for coverings.

 S'mores is a plural word that actually means "some mores." It has been a favorite camp treat for many years.

 About 28% of the American population went camping in 2003. However, it is estimated that only about 6% walked more than a quarter of a mile from their car to make a camp.

 When a hiker is backpacking for long distances, the combined weight that is being carried should not exceed 25% of the hiker's weight, for an average hiker. This weight includes the backpack itself.

 Some of the national parks most often visited by campers include the Great Smokey Mountains, Blue Ridge Mountains, Grand Canyon, and Yosemite.

Three Cheers for June and July PreK–K, SV 9826-4

Sack Backpacks

Materials

- large paper grocery bags
- scissors
- markers
- stapler

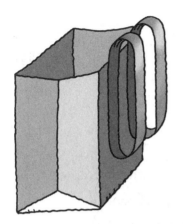

Directions

Teacher Preparation: Cut four inches off the top of each bag. Cut each four-inch strip in half to make two straps. Staple the straps on one side of the bag. Provide a bag for each child.

1. Decorate the outside of the bag with pictures of things that people need when they go camping.

2. Try on your backpack!

Tube Binoculars

Materials

- cardboard tubes
- tape
- foil
- scissors
- yarn
- ruler
- hole punch

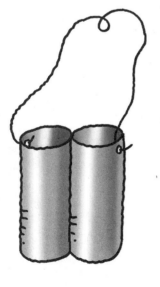

Directions

Teacher Preparation: If using long tubes, cut them down to between four and five inches. Each child will need two tubes.

1. Tape two tubes together.

2. Wrap the joined tubes in foil, folding any overhang into the openings so that the ends are uncovered.

3. Punch a hole, about one-half inch from the top, on each side.

4. Wrap a piece of yarn around the length of a ruler (24 inches) and cut the yarn.

5. Tie each end of the yarn through a hole.

Solar S'mores

You will need

- graham crackers
- large marshmallows
- chocolate bars
- foil

Note: This activity needs to be enjoyed on a hot, sunny day.

Directions

Teacher Preparation: Find a place outside that is directly in the sun for several hours. Make sure the area will remain free of insects while the s'mores are "cooking."

1. Break a graham cracker in half.

2. Tear off a large piece of foil and lay the cracker half in the center.

3. Place part of a chocolate bar on the cracker.

4. Place a marshmallow on the chocolate.

5. Place the other half of the cracker on the marshmallow.

6. Wrap the foil around the sandwich so that it is completely covered.

7. Place the foil in a sunny spot for an hour.

Note: Be aware of children who may have food allergies.

Three Cheers for June and July PreK–K, SV 9826-4

♫ A-camping We Will Go!

(Tune: "Hi, Ho, the Dairy-o")

A-camping we will go.

A-camping we will go.

Grab your tent and sleeping bag!

A-camping we will go!

A-hiking we will go.

A-hiking we will go.

Grab your pack and binoculars!

A-hiking we will go!

A-canoeing we will go.

A-canoeing we will go.

Grab your boat and paddle, too!

A-canoeing we will go!

Paddle Toward These Books

Amelia Bedelia Goes Camping
by Peggy Parish (HarperTrophy)

Angelina and Henry
by Katharine Holabird (Pleasant Company)

Curious George Goes Camping
by H. A. Rey (Houghton Mifflin)

Henry and Mudge Go Camping
by Cynthia Rylant
(Simon & Schuster Children's Publishing)

I Can Go Hiking
by Edna Eckart (Children's Press)

Just Me and My Dad
by Mercer Mayer (Western Publishing)

Maisy Goes Camping
by Lucy Cousins (Candlewick Press)

Three Days on a River in a Red Canoe
by Vera B. Williams (HarperTrophy)

A-camping We Will Go!

Materials

- pattern on page 53
- markers
- green craft paper
- border
- scissors
- stapler
- glue
- brown, green, and white construction paper
- yarn (to match the color of children's hair)

Directions

Teacher Preparation: Duplicate the tent pattern on brown and white construction paper. Cover the board with the craft paper. Add trees cut out of brown and green construction paper. Add a festive border and the caption. Cut out a three-inch circle from white paper for each child.

1. Draw a face on the circle.

2. Cut yarn for hair and glue it around the face.

3. Cut out a brown and a white tent.

4. Cut along the dotted lines of the brown tent to make a door.

5. Fold the flap back on each side.

6. Place the brown tent over the white tent so that the edges match.

7. Slide the face between the paper tents so that it will show through the opened door of the brown tent.

8. Glue the face to the white tent.

9. Glue the white and brown tent together, making sure the door can open and close.

Help children staple their tents to the bulletin board.

Three Cheers for June and July PreK–K, SV 9826-4

Camping Centers

Language Center

Language Arts Standard
Identifies beginning sounds

Sounds Like Camping Fun

Materials

- scissors
- construction paper
- picture cards on page 51
- glue
- crayons

Teacher Preparation: Duplicate the eight picture cards.

Have children color and cut apart the cards. Tell children that these are pictures of things they would see on a camping trip. Have children pair the pictures whose names begin with the same sound. Have children glue the pairs on construction paper.

Math Center

Math Standard
Creates a simple graph that uses pictures

Camping Graph

Materials

- crayons
- activity master on page 52

Teacher Preparation: Duplicate the activity master and provide one for each child.

Have children identify the shapes as they color the picture. Then have them count the shapes and color a box in the graph for each shape they counted.

Camping Centers

Writing Center

Science Standard
Observes and describes properties of objects

Who's in the Tent?

Materials

- construction paper
- recycled magazines
- pattern on page 53
- glue
- crayons
- scissors

Teacher Preparation: Duplicate the tent pattern. Provide a pattern for each child.

Have children color and cut out the tent. Then have them cut along the dotted line to make the tent door. Ask children to find and cut out a magazine picture of something they would put in a tent. Next, have children glue the cutout picture to the bottom center of a sheet of construction paper. Help children glue the tent on the construction paper so that the object can be seen under the flap. Have children dictate or write three clues that describe the item in their tent. Allow children to take turns reading the clues and guessing the object.

Science Center

Science Standard
Explores science through the use of the five senses

Sensing in Nature

Materials

- crayons
- activity master on page 54

Teacher Preparation: Duplicate the activity master. Provide an activity master for each child.

Discuss how children learn about the world by seeing, hearing, smelling, tasting, and touching. Have children color the pictures. Then have children cirlce all the senses they would use to learn about each item.

Camping Centers

Dramatic Play Center

Social Studies Standard
Identifies customs and traditions

Camping Fun

Materials

- animal pictures
- self-standing tent
- large, clean rocks
- camping equipment
- red, yellow, orange, brown tempera paints
- binoculars and backpacks completed in "Tube Binoculars" and "Sack Backpacks" on page 43
- tape
- newspaper
- paintbrushes
- sleeping bags

Teacher Preparation: Roll newspaper into tubes and tape closed. Paint the tubes to look like burning logs. Use the rocks to make a fire ring and stack the painted logs in the center. Set up the camping equipment. Tape the animal pictures to the wall.

Invite children to pretend they are camping. They can cook over the fire, go hiking with backpacks, use their binoculars to look for animals, and sleep in the tent.

Game Center

Math Standard
Applies and adapts a variety of strategies to solve problems

Hiking Trails

Materials

- pattern on page 55
- 3 file folders
- markers
- scissors
- glue
- washable markers
- squirt bottles filled with water
- paper towels

Teacher Preparation: Duplicate three maze activity masters. Draw a picture of a rock or tree branch across several paths so that there is only one solution for each maze. Make each maze different. Glue a maze to the inside of a file folder and laminate.

Have children use washable markers to help the hikers get back to camp. Encourage children to wipe the game board clean when they are finished.

Camping Centers

Art Center

Math Standard
Applies and adapts a variety of strategies to solve problems

Canoe for You

Materials

- hole punch
- pattern on page 56
- construction paper in a variety of colors
- yarn
- scissors
- markers

Teacher Preparation: Duplicate the canoe pattern on the construction paper.

Have children cut out the canoe and fold it along the dotted line. Then have them punch holes as indicated and thread yarn through the holes to sew the sides of the canoe together. Invite children to use markers to decorate their canoes.

Block Center

Science Standard
Understands the position and motion of objects

Along the River

Materials

- scissors
- blue felt
- canoes completed in "Canoe for You" on page 50

Teacher Preparation: Cut the felt into the shape of a long river.

Invite children to build a river to canoe on. They can stack blocks at varying heights to make falls and rapids. Have children move their canoes along the river.

Camping Picture Cards

Use with "Sounds Like Camping Fun" on page 47.

tent

fire

canoe

tree

canteen

backpack

fox

bird

Three Cheers for June and July PreK–K, SV 9826-4

Name _____

Camping Shapes

Directions: Use with "Camping Graph" on page 47. Have children identify the shapes as they color the picture. Then have them count the shapes and color a box in the graph for each shape they counted.

Unit 4, A-camping We Will Go!: Activity Master
Three Cheers for June and July PreK–K, SV 9826-4

Tent Pattern

Use with "A-camping We Will Go!" on page 46 and "Who's in the Tent?" on page 48.

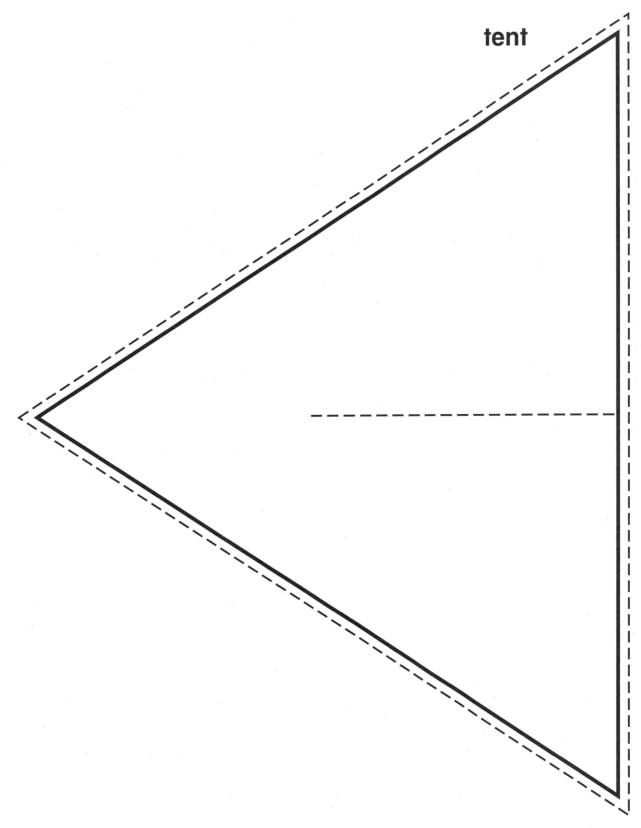

tent

Name

Our Five Senses

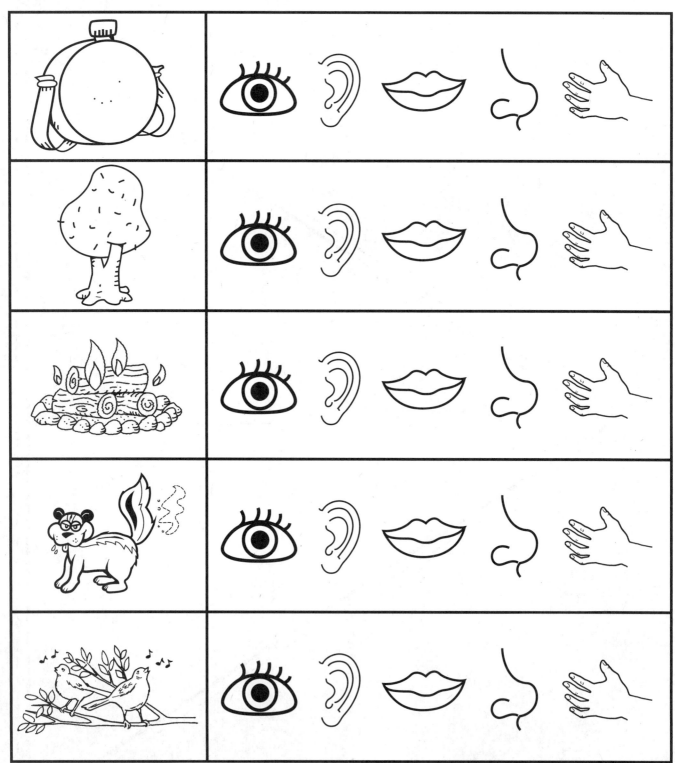

Directions: Use with "Sensing in Nature" on page 48. Have children color the pictures. Then have children circle all the senses they would use to learn about each item.

Unit 4, A-camping We Will Go!: Activity Master
Three Cheers for June and July PreK–K, SV 9826-4

Hiking Trails Pattern

Use with "Hiking Trails" on page 49.

Unit 4, A-camping We Will Go!: Pattern
Three Cheers for June and July PreK–K, SV 9826-4

Canoe Pattern

Use with "Canoe for You" on page 50.

canoe

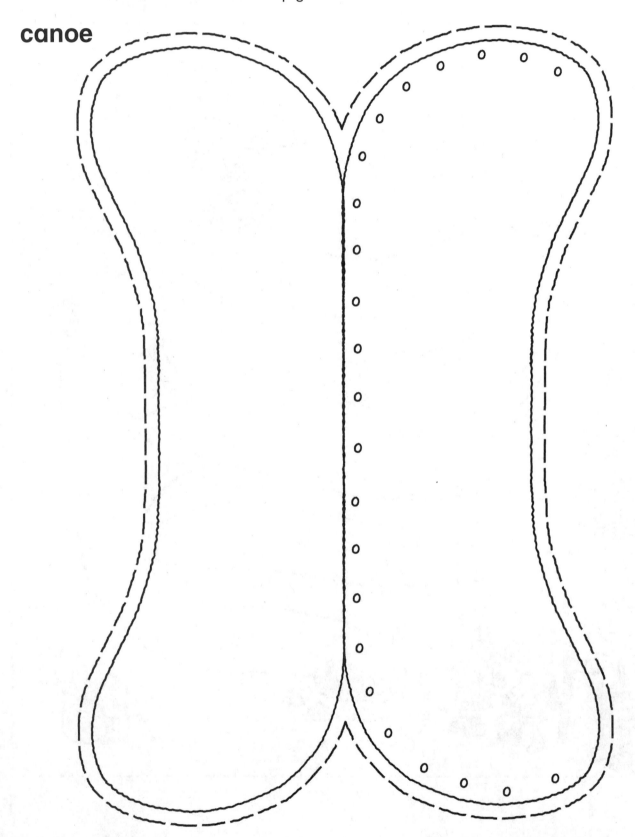

The Little Red Hen

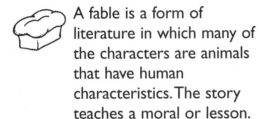 A fable is a form of literature in which many of the characters are animals that have human characteristics. The story teaches a moral or lesson.

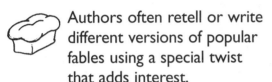 Authors often retell or write different versions of popular fables using a special twist that adds interest.

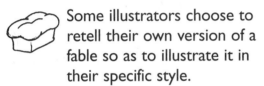 Some illustrators choose to retell their own version of a fable so as to illustrate it in their specific style.

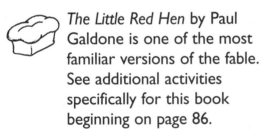 *The Little Red Hen* by Paul Galdone is one of the most familiar versions of the fable. See additional activities specifically for this book beginning on page 86.

 While the plot of *The Little Red Hen* generally stays the same, the lazy animal characters may change.

Likewise, the end product that Red Hen bakes may change. In some stories, she bakes a loaf of bread, a cake, and even a pizza!

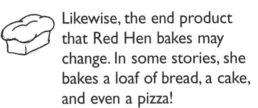

Red Hen Books

Help Yourself, Little Red Hen
by Dr. Alvin Granowsky
(Steck-Vaughn)

The Little Red Hen
by Byron Barton (HarperCollins)

The Little Red Hen
by Paul Galdone (Clarion Books)

The Little Red Hen
by Carol Ottolenghi
(Amer Education Publishers)

The Little Red Hen, An Old Story
by Margot Zemach (Farrer, Straus and Giroux)

The Little Red Hen and the Ear of Wheat
by Mary Finch (Barefoot Books)

Little Red Hen (Makes a Pizza)
by Philemon Sturges
(Dutton Children's Books)

With Love, Little Red Hen
by Alma Flor Ada (Atheneum Books for Young Readers)

Little Red Hen

Materials

- pattern on page 66
- red and yellow construction paper
- red feathers
- scissors
- glue

Directions

Teacher Preparation: Duplicate the hen pattern on red paper. Provide a pattern for each child.

1. Cut out a hen body.
2. Cut out a yellow circle for an eye.
3. Cut out two yellow triangles for a beak.
4. Cut out two more yellow triangles for feet. Cut out two small triangles on each foot to make toes.
5. Glue the parts on the hen body.
6. Glue on feathers for the wing and the tail.

Little Red Hen Character Puppets

Materials

- small lunch bags
- construction paper
- scissors
- glue
- markers
- art supplies, such as red feathers, pipe cleaners, fabric scraps

Directions

1. Choose a favorite character from *The Little Red Hen*.
2. Cut out or draw the body parts to make the puppet.
3. Glue on the cutout parts.
4. Use the art supplies to add more details to the puppet.

Little Red Hen Breadsticks

You will need

- frozen dough rolls
- flour
- beaten egg
- Parmesan cheese
- wax-paper squares
- pastry brush
- cookie sheets
- oven

Directions

Teacher Preparation: Defrost the rolls according to the directions. After children have placed their breadsticks on the cookie sheet, bake them in a 350°F oven until lightly browned.

1. Spread a little flour on a wax-paper square.
2. Make a 6-inch snake from a defrosted roll by rolling it on the wax paper.
3. Brush with the beaten egg.
4. Sprinkle with the cheese.
5. Move the wax paper to the cookie sheet.

Note: Be aware of children who may have food allergies.

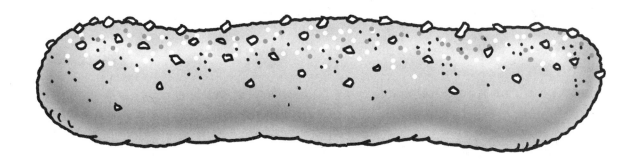

♫ Like the Little Red Hen

(Tune: "Row, Row, Row Your Boat")

Plant, plant, plant a seed,   (Pretend to plant seeds.)
Like the Little Red Hen.
I'll help you, and you'll help me.   (Shake hands with a partner.)
Then we can eat some bread!   (Rub stomach.)

Cut, cut, cut the wheat,   (Pretend to cut wheat stalks.)
Like the Little Red Hen.
I'll help you, and you'll help me.   (Shake hands with a partner.)
Then we can eat some bread!   (Rub stomach.)

Beat, beat, beat the wheat,   (Pretend to beat wheat stalks.)
Like the Little Red Hen.
I'll help you, and you'll help me.   (Shake hands with a partner.)
Then we can eat some bread!   (Rub stomach.)

Mill, mill, mill the wheat,   (Pretend to grind wheat seeds.)
Like the Little Red Hen.
I'll help you, and you'll help me.   (Shake hands with a partner.)
Then we can eat some bread!   (Rub stomach.)

Knead, knead, knead the bread,   (Pretend to knead bread dough.)
Like the Little Red Hen.
I'll help you, and you'll help me.   (Shake hands with a partner.)
Then we can eat some bread!   (Rub stomach.)

Bake, bake, bake the bread,   (Pretend to put bread in the oven.)
Like the Little Red Hen.
I'll help you, and you'll help me.   (Shake hands with a partner.)
Then we can eat some bread!   (Rub stomach.)

Eat, eat, eat the bread,   (Pretend to eat bread.)
Like the Little Red Hen.
I helped you, and you helped me.   (Shake hands with a partner.)
Now we can share the bread!   (Rub stomach.)

Materials

- hens completed in "Little Red Hen" on page 58
- pattern on page 67
- craft paper
- markers
- pencils
- scissors
- border
- stapler

Directions

Teacher Preparation: Duplicate the speech bubble pattern. Cover the board with the craft paper. Draw a background scene of a farm with markers. Staple the hens in a pleasing design on the board, leaving space for the speech bubbles. Add a festive border and the caption.

1. Write or dictate words to complete the sentence frame to tell what you can do to help in school.

2. Cut out the speech bubble.

3. Staple the speech bubble next to your hen.

Red Hen Centers

Math Center

Math Standard
Matches objects to
outlines of shapes

Character Matching

Materials

- white craft paper
- patterns on page 68
- markers and crayons
- scissors

Teacher Preparation: Enlarge and duplicate *The Little Red Hen* character patterns. Color and cut them out. Trace the outlines on the craft paper.

Invite children to name the characters from *The Little Red Hen*. Then have children match each character to its outline.

Language Center

Language Arts Standard
Recognizes uppercase and
lowercase letters

Letter Match

Materials

- 2 file folders
- crayons or markers
- patterns on page 69
- glue
- scissors

Teacher Preparation: Make 12 copies each of the hen and cake patterns. Color and cut them out. Write a capital letter on each hen and a matching lowercase letter on each cake. Glue six hens on the inside of each file folder.

Invite children to place a cake on a hen to match the partner letters.

Red Hen Centers

Dramatic Play Center

Language Arts Standard
Sequences events accurately

Story Retelling

Materials

- craft sticks
- patterns on page 68
- white construction paper
- glue
- sheet
- scissors
- markers or crayons
- large box
- clothesline

Teacher Preparation: Duplicate, color, and cut out the characters in the Little Red Hen story you shared with the children. Glue the pictures to craft sticks to make puppets. Draw and cut out a seed, wheat, flour bag, cake, or other important story parts to make prop puppets for the story retelling. Set up a puppet theater using a large box or a sheet draped over a clothesline.

Invite children to retell the story of *The Little Red Hen* using the puppets and props.

Reading Center

Language Arts Standard
Develops awareness of story elements, such as character, setting, problem, and solution

Compare Stories

Materials

- several versions of *The Little Red Hen* (See list on page 57.)

Challenge partners to look at the different books and find ways that the stories are alike and different.

Red Hen Centers

Sensory Center

Social Studies Standard
Understands how people lived in earlier times

Grinding Wheat

Materials

- tub
- grass seed
- mortar and pestle (or large flat rock and small round rock)

Teacher Preparation: Put some grass seed in the tub. Place the grinding tools in the tub, too.

Remind children that the Little Red Hen took the wheat to the mill to be ground into flour. Then explain that a long time ago, all people took wheat they grew to the mill to have flour made. Invite children to grind the seed into a flour-like powder with the tools.

Block Center

Social Studies Standard
Follows rules, such as sharing and taking turns

Working Together

Materials

- blocks

Discuss what might have happened if the characters in *The Little Red Hen* had worked together to grow the wheat and make the bread or cake. Then talk about why it is important to help each other. Challenge all the children in the group to work together to build a tall structure with the blocks.

Red Hen Centers

Writing Center

Language Arts Standard
Makes illustrations to match stories

Baking Up Some Fun

Materials

- crayons
- activity master on page 70

Teacher Preparation: Duplicate the "Baking Fun" activity master. Provide a copy for each child.

Have children write or dictate the name of a food they would bake if they were the Little Red Hen. Then have them draw a picture of the food.

Science Center

Science Standard
Performs experiments with materials to notice change

Yea for Yeast!

Materials

- quick-rise yeast
- measuring spoons
- small, clear plastic cups
- sugar
- thermos
- warm water

Teacher Preparation: Fill the thermos with warm tap water. Make a rebus poster to show that children mix one teaspoon of yeast, one-fourth teaspoon of sugar, and one tablespoon of warm thermos water in a cup.

Explain that bread, cake, pizza dough, and many other bakery treats use yeast to help them grow bigger. Then invite partners to follow the rebus chart to mix the ingredients to see how yeast works. Ask children to check the mixture several times during an hour.

Hen Pattern

Use with "Little Red Hen" on page 58.

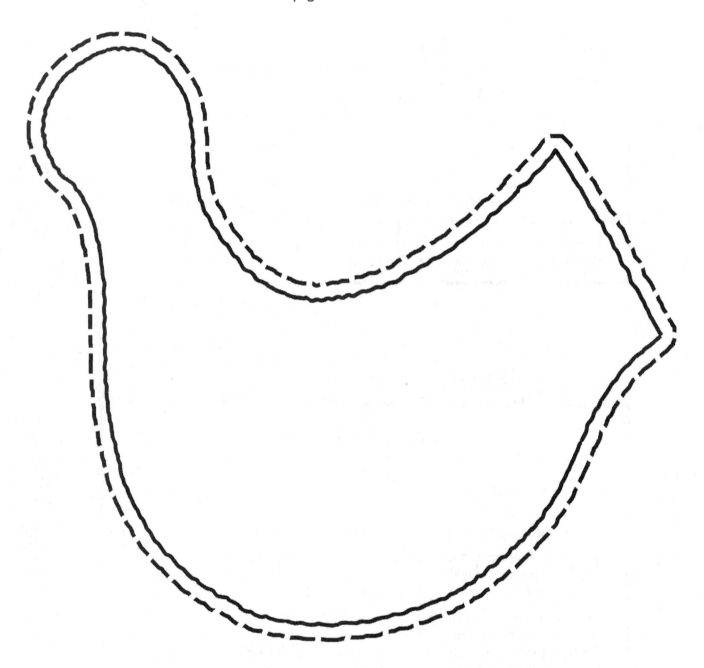

Three Cheers for June and July PreK–K, SV 9826-4

Speech Bubble Pattern

Use with "Red Hen Helpers" on page 61.

I can help

_____

- - - - - - - - - - - - - - - - -

_____

Character Patterns

Use with "Character Matching" on page 62 and "Story Retelling" on page 63.

Three Cheers for June and July PreK–K, SV 9826-4

Hen and Cake Patterns

Use with "Letter Match" on page 62.

Three Cheers for June and July PreK–K, SV 9826-4

Name _____

Baking Fun

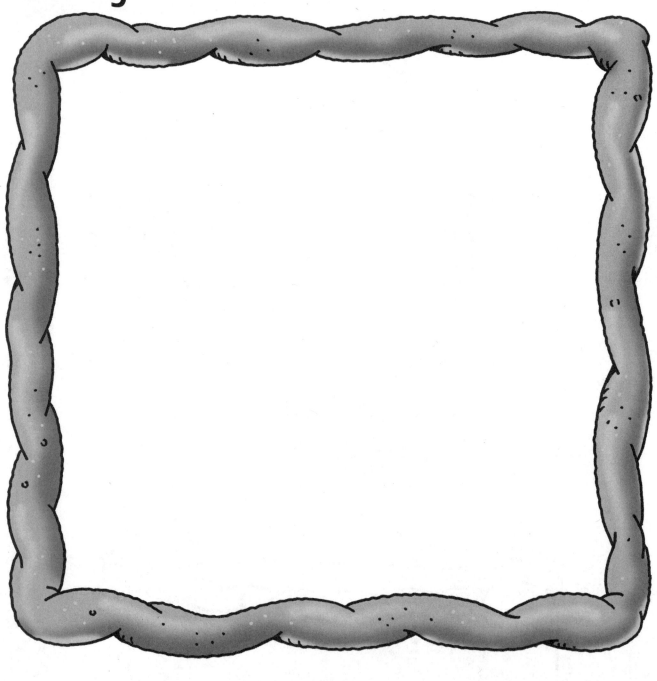

I will bake a _____.

Directions: Use with "Baking Up Some Fun" on page 65. Have children write or dictate the name of a food they would bake if they were the Little Red Hen. Then have them draw a picture of the food.

Unit 5, The Little Red Hen: Activity Master
Three Cheers for June and July PreK–K, SV 9826-4

Show Your Independence

 Independence Day is also known as July Fourth and the birthday of the United States of America.

 Independence Day is a holiday in the United States that celebrates the adoption of the *Declaration of Independence* by the Continental Congress on July 4, 1776.

 The *Declaration* was really signed on July 8, 1776, in Philadelphia, Pennsylvania. On this day the people in the United States actually celebrated the very first Independence Day with songs, the ringing of the Liberty Bell, a parade, and the firing of cannons.

 The first official flag was ordered in 1777. It was to have seven red and six white alternating stripes, which stood for the 13 colonies that signed the *Declaration of Independence*. It was to also have 13 stars on a field of blue to represent that a new constellation had been formed.

 Militiamen returning from the American Revolution continued the tradition of celebrating with parades, cannon fire, and music each year.

 Fireworks take the place of cannon fire today.

 The *Star-Spangled Banner*, the anthem of the United States, was written by Francis Scott Key during the Battle Over Baltimore on September 12–14, 1812. It was actually written as a poem.

 The flag has several names: Stars and Stripes, Old Glory, and Star-Spangled Banner.

 Independence Day was set aside as a national holiday in 1941.

 One of the largest Independence Day celebrations happens in Washington, D.C. Over 300,000 people watch a parade that passes the White House, the home of the United States President.

Three Cheers for June and July PreK–K, SV 9826-4

Parade Floats

Materials

- patterns on page 80
- shoe boxes
- craft sticks
- yarn
- red, white, and blue construction paper
- markers
- scissors
- hole punch
- glue

Directions

Teacher Preparation: Duplicate the American symbols patterns. Punch two holes in one end of each shoe box. Cut several slits in the bottom of each box wide enough for a craft stick. Cut three-inch strips of red, white, and blue construction paper.

1. Turn a box over so the bottom is face up.

2. Fringe strips of construction paper and glue them to all four sides of the box to make a float.

3. Color and cut out the American symbols.

4. Draw and cut out a picture of yourself.

5. Draw and cut out pictures of other people and things to ride on your float.

6. Glue the pictures to craft sticks or to the sides of the float.

7. Push each craft stick in a slit to make it stand.

8. Cut a long piece of yarn. Weave it through both holes at the end of the box to make a pull handle. Tie the ends together.

July Fourth Sparklers

Materials

- straws
- rulers
- scissors
- tape
- ¼-inch sparkling gift ribbons in various colors

Directions

1. Choose a ribbon color. Cut a piece of ribbon that is as long as a ruler.

2. Repeat with nine more colors of ribbon.

3. Tape the ribbons to the end of a straw.

4. Wave the sparklers while marching to music.

Note: Play patriotic music on a portable player and invite children to march in a parade through the hallway. They can wave their sparklers and pull their floats as they celebrate the birthday of the United States of America.

Red, White, and Blue Yogurt Cups

You will need

- vanilla yogurt
- blueberries
- strawberries
- bananas
- plastic knives and spoons
- half-cup measure
- plastic cups
- plastic cutting board

Directions

Teacher Preparation: Cut the bananas into fourths.

1. Measure a half cup of yogurt into a plastic cup.

2. Count out five blueberries and put them on the yogurt.

3. Get a piece of a banana and peel it. Cut it into slices. Put it on the yogurt.

4. Get a strawberry. Cut it into slices. Put it on the yogurt, too.

5. Stir the fruit into the yogurt.

Note: Be aware of children who may have food allergies.

♫ Independence Day Fun Chant

Pack a picnic and watch a parade.

Stand when our flag goes by.

Then late at night you can go to the park

And watch the fireworks fly in the sky.

Festive Fourth Books

This Land Is Your Land
by Woodie Guthrie (Little, Brown, and Company)

Parade
by Donald Crews (Mulberry)

Apple Pie Fourth of July
by Janet S. Wong (Harcourt Children's Books)

The Story of America's Birthday
by Patricia A. Pingry (Candy Cane Press)

Hats Off for the Fourth of July
by Harriet Ziefert (Viking)

The Star-Spangled Banner
by Peter Spier (Yearling Books)

America the Beautiful
by Lucy Cousins (Candlewick Press)

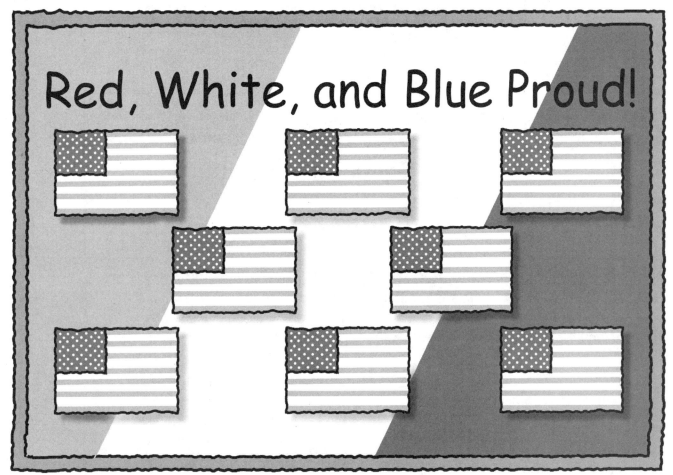

Red, White, and Blue Proud!

Materials

- red, white, and blue construction paper
- self-stick, gold foil stars
- red, white, and blue craft paper
- border
- scissors
- stapler
- glue

Directions

Teacher Preparation: Cut red construction paper into half-inch lengthwise strips for the flag's stripes. Cut blue construction paper into four-inch by five-inch rectangles for the blue field. Then cut the craft paper into angled stripes and staple it to the bulletin board to make the background. Add the caption and a border.

1. Glue seven red stripes on white construction paper to make the stripes of the flag.

2. Glue the blue rectangle in the top left corner of the flag.

3. Place 50 stars on the blue rectangle.

Help children staple their flags to the bulletin board. Ask them to describe a pattern they see on the flag. Discuss what it means to be proud.

Independence Centers

Language Center

Language Arts Standard
Recognizes lowercase letters

Here Comes the Band!

Materials

- crayons or markers
- activity master on page 81

Teacher Preparation: Duplicate the "Musical Letters" activity master.

Have children circle the letters in each row that are the same as the first letter.

Math Center

Math Standard
Reads and orders whole numbers up to 10

Parade Lineup

Materials

- sentence strips
- cards on pages 82 and 83
- crayons
- scissors
- glue

Teacher Preparation: Duplicate the "Parade Number Line" cards.

Have children color and cut apart the floats. Then ask them to glue the floats on a sentence strip in numerical order.

Independence Centers

Writing Center

Social Studies Standard
Identifies customs associated with holidays

Holiday Class Book

Materials

- hole punch
- construction paper
- activity master on page 84
- pencil
- binder
- crayons

Teacher Preparation: Duplicate the "Independence Day Fun" activity master on construction paper. Make a cover with a title "Independence Day Fun" and bind the completed pages together to make a class book.

Invite children to write or dictate an ending to the sentence frame. Then have them draw a picture to illustrate the sentence.

Block Center

Math Standard
Creates and extends a simple pattern involving color and shape

Patriotic Color Patterns

Materials

- red, white, and blue pattern blocks

Ask children to create color and/or shape patterns using the blocks. Then have them challenge a friend to continue the pattern.

Independence Centers

Sensory Center

Math Standard
Sorts or classifies by color

Color Sorting

Materials

- rotini pasta
- paper towels
- rubbing alcohol
- red and blue food coloring
- bowls
- spoons
- large tub

Teacher Preparation: Allow one week to dye and dry the pasta. Pour a cup of rubbing alcohol into each of two bowls. Add red food color to one bowl to make a deep red color and add blue food color to the other bowl. Divide the dry pasta into three equal amounts. Pour one third of the pasta into the red bowl and one third into the blue bowl. Stir the pasta to coat and continue to stir it for several days. When the pasta is a deep color, drain the alcohol and let the noodles dry on paper towels. Pour all three colors, red, white, and blue, into a large tub.

Invite children to sort the pasta into separate colors.

Game Center

Social Studies Standard
Recognizes national symbols

American Symbols Concentration

Materials

- index cards
- patterns on page 80
- white construction paper
- glue
- scissors
- markers

Teacher Preparation: Duplicate two copies of the "American Symbols" patterns on construction paper. Color and cut out the pictures. Then glue the pictures on index cards to make game cards.

Review the pictures on the cards and explain why they are important American symbols. Then invite children to play a game of Concentration.

Independence Centers

Art Center

Social Studies Standard
Identifies customs associated with holidays

Sky-High Fireworks

Materials

- spoons
- paper plates
- black construction paper
- glue
- glitter

Teacher Preparation: Pour a small amount of each color of glitter into a plate.

Discuss fireworks safety. Invite children to make fireworks explosions and squiggles they might see in the sky. Have them make one image at a time with a thin glue line on black paper. Then have them spoon glitter to cover the glue. Ask them to shake the excess glitter off in the appropriate plate to keep the colors separated before beginning the next sky-high firework.

Block Center

Social Studies Standard
Uses a map

Find That State

Materials

- tracing paper
- large United States map
- tape
- pencils

Teacher Preparation: Tape the map to the wall.

Invite children to locate the water and land areas on the map. Then challenge them to locate their state. Have them trace the outline of the state and write the name of it on the paper. Challenge children to use blocks to make the shape of their state. Discuss the Fourth of July celebrations that take place in your state or your city or town.

American Symbols

Use with "Parade Floats" on page 72 and "American Symbols Concentration" on page 78.

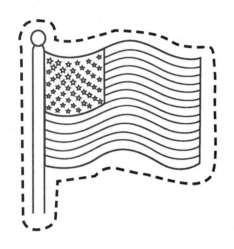

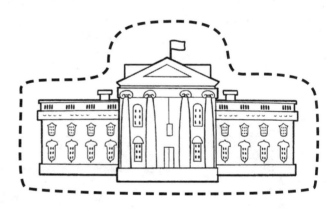

Unit 6, Fourth, Flags, and Fun: Patterns

Three Cheers for June and July PreK–K, SV 9826-4

Name _____

Musical Letters

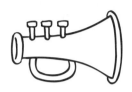

| m | m | m | n |

| p | g | p | p |

| c | c | e | c |

| i | l | i | i |

| n | r | r | r |

| u | u | u | n |

Directions: Use with "Here Comes the Band!" on page 76. Have children circle the letters in each row that are the same as the first letter.

Unit 6, Fourth, Flags, and Fun: Activity Master
Three Cheers for June and July PreK–K, SV 9826-4

Parade Number Line

Use with "Parade Lineup" on page 76.

Unit 6, Fourth, Flags, and Fun: Cards
Three Cheers for June and July PreK–K, SV 9826-4

Parade Number Line

Use with "Parade Lineup" on page 76.

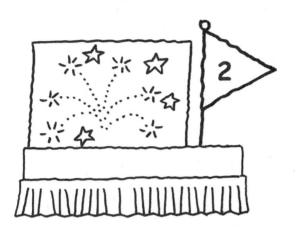

Unit 6, Fourth, Flags, and Fun: Cards
Three Cheers for June and July PreK–K, SV 9826-4

Name _____

Independence Day Fun

On Independence Day, I like to _____

_____

_____.

Directions: Use with "Holiday Class Book" on page 77. Invite children to write or dictate an ending to the sentence frame. Then have them draw a picture to illustrate the sentence.

A Look at Paul Galdone

 Paul Galdone was a well-known children's author and illustrator who was born in Budapest, Hungary, on June 2, 1914.

 He immigrated to the United States when he was 14.

 After going to art school, Paul Galdone worked in a publishing company.

 He illustrated over 300 books, many of which he authored or retold.

 Paul enjoyed using bright colors and action-filled pictures in his stories.

 Paul Galdone won many awards and honors for his books and illustrations, including *Anatole, Anatole and the Cat,* and *The Gingerbread Boy.*

 He died in 1986.

The Little Red Hen
by Paul Galdone (Clarion)

Read *The Little Red Hen* aloud to children. Then invite them to do the following activities.

Growing Wheat

Materials

- cards on page 89
- sentence strips
- crayons
- scissors
- glue

Directions

Teacher Preparation: Duplicate the "From Seed to Cake" cards for each child.

Ask children to color and cut out the pictures that show the sequence of steps from wheat seed to cake. Have them glue the pictures in order on a sentence strip.

Friends Help Friends

Materials

- crayons
- activity master on page 90

Directions

Teacher Preparation: Duplicate the "Good Friends" activity master.

Lead children in a discussion of characteristics that make a good friend. Then ask them if the cat, dog, and mouse were good friends to Red Hen. Ask how the animals changed at the end of the book. Then invite children to write or dictate an ending to the sentence frame to tell what makes a good friend. Have them draw a picture to illustrate the sentence.

Books by Paul Galdone

- *Anatole* (McGraw Hill) (illustrated)

- *Basil of Baker Street* (Pocket Books) (illustrated)

- *Cat Goes Fiddle-I-Fee* (Clarion) (written and illustrated)

- *George Washington's Breakfast* (Puffin) (illustrated)
  This book could accompany the Fourth, Flags, and Fun unit.

- *The Gingerbread Boy* (Clarion) (written and illustrated)

- *Henny Penny* (Clarion) (written and illustrated)

- *The Little Red Hen* (Clarion) (written and illustrated)
  This book could accompany the Little Red Hen unit.

- *The Monkey and the Crocodile: A Jataka Tale* (Clarion) (written and illustrated)

- *The Owl and the Pussy Cat* (Clarion) (written and illustrated)

- *The Three Billy Goats Gruff* (Clarion) (written and illustrated)

- *The Teeny-Tiny Woman* (Clarion) (written and illustrated)

- *Three Little Kittens* (Dragonfly) (written and illustrated)

Unit 7, Author Study: Book List
Three Cheers for June and July PreK–K, SV 9826-4

Bookmark Patterns

Even trolls like to read Paul Galdone's books!

Sail away with Paul Galdone when you read *The Owl and the Pussy Cat.*

Run, run as fast as you can . . . to catch a delicious book by Paul Galdone!

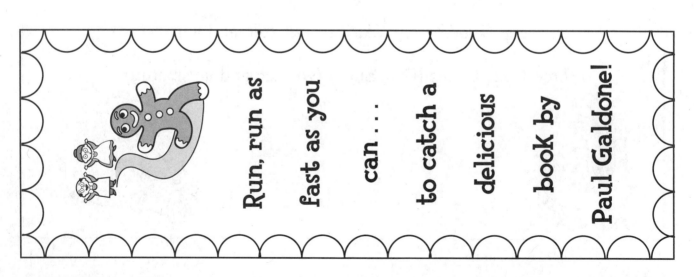

From Seed to Cake

Use with "Growing Wheat" on page 86.

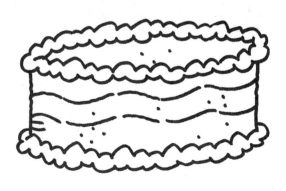

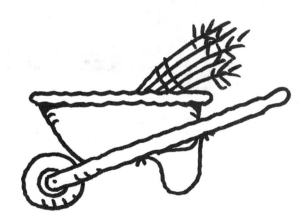

Unit 7, Author Study: Cards
Three Cheers for June and July PreK–K, SV 9826-4

Name _____

Good Friends

A good friend _____.

Directions: Use with "Friends Help Friends" on page 86. Invite children to write or dictate an ending to the sentence frame to tell what makes a good friend. Have them draw a picture to illustrate the sentence.

Unit 7, Author Study: Activity Master
Three Cheers for June and July PreK–K, SV 9826-4

Center Icons

Art Center

Block Center

Dramatic Play Center

Game Center

Center Icons Patterns
Three Cheers for June and July PreK–K, SV 9826-4

Center Icons

Language Center

Math Center

Music Center

Puzzle Center

Center Icons

Reading Center

Science Center

Sensory Center

Writing Center

Student Awards

Congratulations!
You are shining in

_____
- - - - - - - - - - - - - - - -
_____
_____
- - - - - - - - - - - - - - - - .

Child's name

_____
Teacher's signature

_____
Date

Congratulations,

_____
- - - - - - - - - - - - - - - -
_____ .

Child's name

You are the
Student of the Month for

_____
- - - - - - - - - - - - - - - -
_____ .

_____
Teacher's signature

_____
Date

Student Awards Patterns
Three Cheers for June and July PreK–K, SV 9826-4

June Student Award

Child's name

made a splash in

Teacher's signature

Date

June Calendar Day Pattern

Suggested Uses

- Reproduce one card for each day of the month. Write a numeral on each card and place it on your class calendar. Use cards to mark special days.
- Reproduce to make cards to use in word ladders or word walls.
- Reproduce to make cards and write a letter on each card. Children use the cards to form words.
- Reproduce to make cards to create matching or concentration games for students to use in activity centers. Choose from the following possible matching skills or create your own:
  — uppercase and lowercase letters
  — pictures of objects whose names rhyme, have the same beginning or ending sounds, contain short or long vowels
  — pictures of adult animals and baby animals
  — numerals and pictures of objects
  — number words and numerals
  — colors and shapes
  — high-frequency sight words

Three Cheers for June and July PreK–K, SV 9826-4

July Student Award

_____

Child's name

was a "stars and stripes" student in

_____

_____

Teacher's signature   **Date**

July Calendar Day Pattern

Suggested Uses

- Reproduce one card for each day of the month. Write a numeral on each card and place it on your class calendar. Use cards to mark special days.
- Reproduce to make cards to use in word ladders or word walls.
- Reproduce to make cards and write a letter on each card. Children use the cards to form words.
- Reproduce to make cards to create matching or concentration games for students to use in activity centers. Choose from the following possible matching skills or create your own:
  - uppercase and lowercase letters
  - pictures of objects whose names rhyme, have the same beginning or ending sounds, contain short or long vowels
  - pictures of adult animals and baby animals
  - numerals and pictures of objects
  - number words and numerals
  - colors and shapes
  - high-frequency sight words